I0485131

How To:
Organize Your Photo Library
in 7 Easy Steps

The first in a series about

Personal Information Management

by

PETER GAILEY

The PIM Coach

www.PIMCoach.com

PIM Coach PRESS

First edition

Library of Congress Control number: TBD

International Standard Book Numbers ISBN:

Soft cover 978-0-9855297-0-3

Ebook 978-0-9855297-0-3

Foreword

"I am in the Real Estate business. I can't tell you how many of my clients dread the fact that they have to needlessly move boxes and boxes of memorabilia around in their moves. Peter Gailey's book, *HOW TO: Organize Your Photo Library* **In 7 Easy Steps** provides great advice about cutting the clutter in your life and would greatly reduce the number of boxes that have to be moved.

Many of my clients are downsizing, and getting their pictures on a CD or a DVD would reduce their work load, simplify their life and give them the opportunity to enjoy their memories.

Additionally, I am a HUGE photographer personally. I too have BOXES of family, vacation and memorable events that need to be put on CD's or DVD's. I am taking advantage of this great information."

- Dennis J. O'Hagan, *D* Magazine's "Best Real Estate Agent in Dallas" Award 2010, 2011 & 2012

Peter Gailey

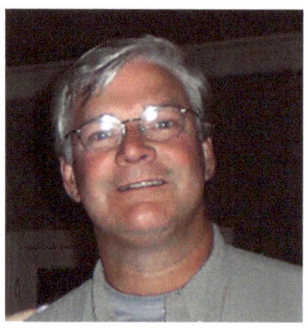 Peter Gailey is recognized globally as the "Personal Information Management Coach". His message is "Tame The Data Deluge" Manage your personal data, or lose it. He has been in the High Tech industry for thirty years and has been instrumental in helping design and specifies some of the world's most trusted and secure systems and data architectures. He has a passion for data and data management. His conclusion: "Personal data is at risk of being lost. We are at a critical crossroad in the evolving history of technology, and services as they relate to Personal Information Management (PIM)". His perspective ranges from the individual to the enterprise.

Managing and preserving data for long periods of time is one of the high tech industry issues that have yet to be solved. Peter has the perspective and experience to help individuals "Manage the Data Deluge" that is engulfing their lives

Dedication

To my wife Robin for her endless patience.
To those with boxes of pictures that are not being enjoyed.
To everyone who needs to "Tame The Data Deluge"
in their personal life.

Preface

Photographs are precious. They represent our lives, our families, our parents, our children growing up, the vacation that was unforgettable, and family reunions. We have preserved everything in our lives in photographs. They are irreplaceable. In fact, other than to save a family member, photograph albums are what draw people back into a burning house more than anything else. They are the things most often looked for when a disaster like a tornado strikes and they are the things most often grieved if they are lost.

Many of us have thousands of pictures we took before the age of the digital camera. If you are like me, you don't want to lose those precious photos and memories. This book will help you organize, convert to a digital format, preserve, and most importantly enjoy your life's most precious memories.

Table of Contents

Introduction

If the pile of pictures you have spread all over your home, looks like the next picture, this book is for you! Note: This is a fraction of my collection of pictures accumulated over 45 years.

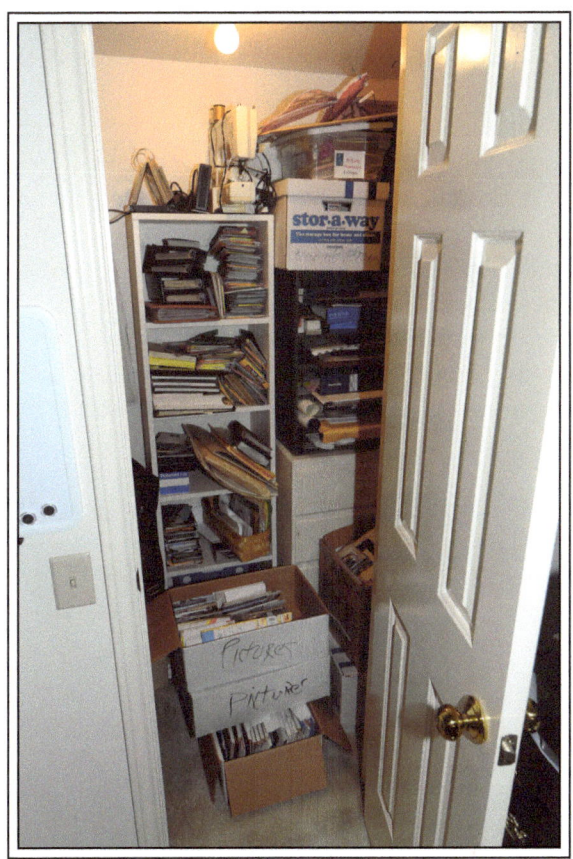

Some Facts about Photography

- Ninety eight percent of all new data is in digital form.
- There is more data being generated in the world than there is media into which it can be stored.
- The photo industry has converted almost entirely to a digital format.
- Most people born after 1990 have never taken a photo using traditional "film."
- Family portraits are currently almost all generated in a digital format.
- Most individuals born before 1985 have hordes of old printed pictures collecting dust and stored away in boxes, probably never to be seen again.
- Sixty four percent of people surveyed by Hewlett Packard (HP) have no process or strategy to save and preserve their precious pictures.

From the author:

Families and individuals have taken and are storing thousands of hard copy pictures. In the past, hard copy pictures were very expensive. Slides were cheaper; so many people 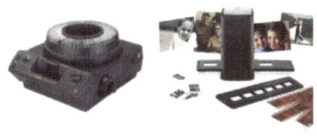 watched slide shows. Slides were replaced by hard copy pictures as the technologies and costs made them more affordable.

In the late 1980s and early 1990s digital pictures overtook printed pictures. Now, with the proliferation of inexpensive digital cameras and high resolution digital camera phones, the world of photography is almost exclusively digital.

We are experiencing an explosion in information and data. With the advent of digital photography and all of its advancements, printed photos are becoming a thing of the past. And quickly. They are at risk for many reasons.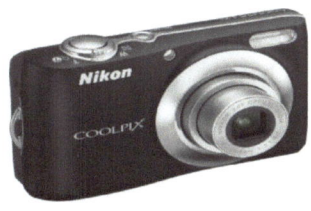

The intent of this book is to help you find, organize and convert your old photos from hard copy to the newest digital format, so your precious pictures can be retained, preserved, shared and most importantly enjoyed.

Peter Gailey – The PIM Coach

1

Get Organized, Get Committed

Whatever your compelling reason is, if you really want to organize and save your photographs, you need to commit to the project. Get help if you can. This book is about giving you a process to help manage all of your pictures, reducing the piles of hard copy pictures and managing your electronic pictures so you can enjoy them as you dreamed of doing when you first took them. It will take a bit of effort, a bit of time and some minor expense, but might also prove to be some fun.

It is best to set aside a space to work. The amounts of time and space will depend on how many photos you have. The amount of expense will depend on how many photos you decide to maintain. This will, more than likely, be a project in which you will need to do the major portions yourself. Only you know the significance of your collection. Consider making this a family project once you have sorted through your pictures.

Notes:

Work Location:

Boxes:

Markers:

Systems needed:

Sources of pictures:

2

Step One: Gather All Your Content

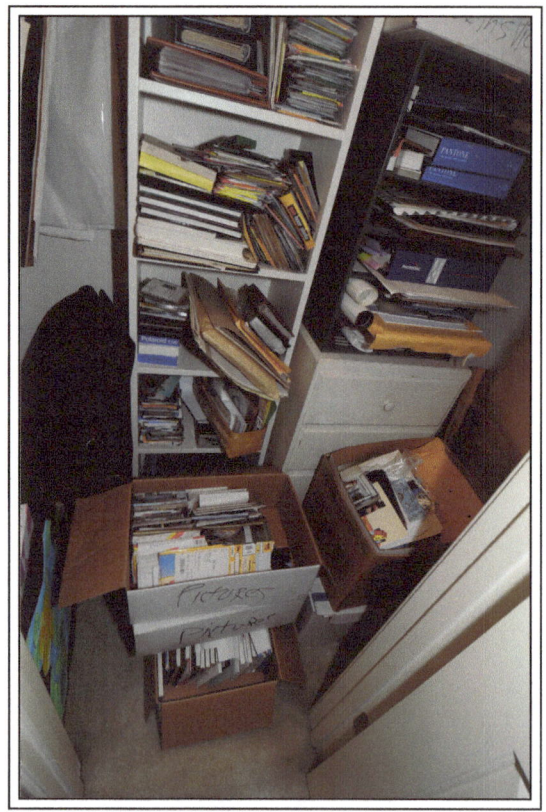

This is a photo of most of the hard copy photos I have accumulated over time.

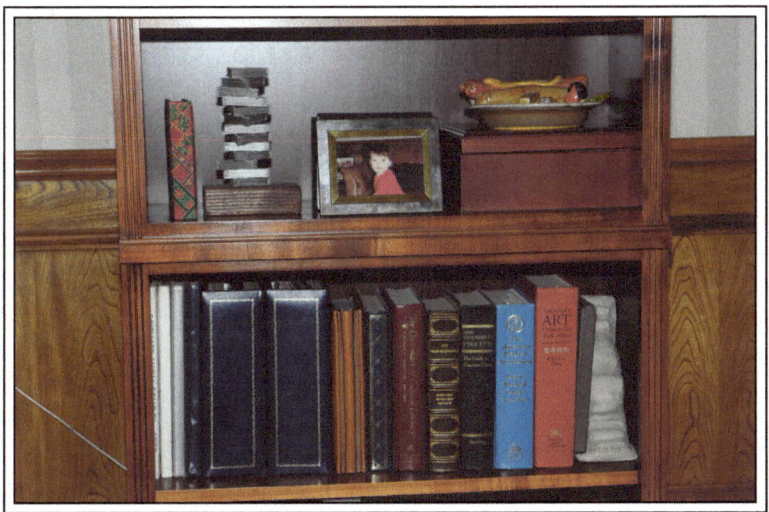

Photo albums

You may find photos in albums, in closets, stored away in drawers and boxes. You'll probably find more than you remember. There may be more than you initially find, but don't worry, finding new ones is half the fun. Consider this project as a journey. You can and will find random pictures over your lifetime. Use the following process to manage your photo library.

> **NOTE:** Special care may be needed for photos already in albums. If you will damage the photo by removing it from the album, think twice about doing this.

3

Step two: Sort Chronologically

Create a Log

Sort all of your photos chronologically. Note the note dividers per year. Create a high level log of this in chronological order. For instance sort by year, then by event within that year. (I put all the pictures in chronological order in a few boxes, and slipped a piece of paper between the yearly breaks.) Call this a high level sort. If you do not know exactly what order they were taken, don't worry about it. Put them in the general vicinity.

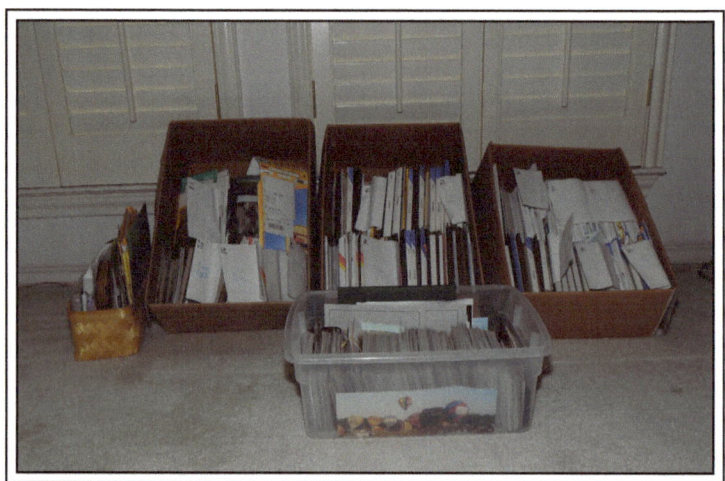

Pictures chronologically sorted.

Files and Log

Years:

Special Events:

Themes:

Topics:

4

Step Three: Fine Tune Each Item

Prioritize and sort the individual pictures. Go through them all. (I suggest you decide on a number of pictures that you would like to maintain and have ready access to forever. 100? 250? 500? 1,000? Only you can decide.) Set these individual pictures aside in chronological order.

Decide up front, what to do with the rest of your pictures. Do you really need eight pictures of that one scene on vacation 15 years ago? Do you really need five big boxes of pictures in storage? Keep the best. Toss the rest! Cut down on the clutter.

NOTE: Tame the data deluge! An important consideration is that over time the best pictures more than likely have already been taken out and are no longer in your collection. These will need to be found and included in this process. For example, my family has our favorites, and we have them located around our home in frames and albums.

Set up four piles: Be Ruthless!!

1. Keepers
2. Delicate Photos
3. Gifting
4. Recycle / Trash

Pile 1: "Keepers" that you want to digitize and have ready access to forever.

Take notice of the development process and the different stages of development in this picture. This is due to the technology at the time.

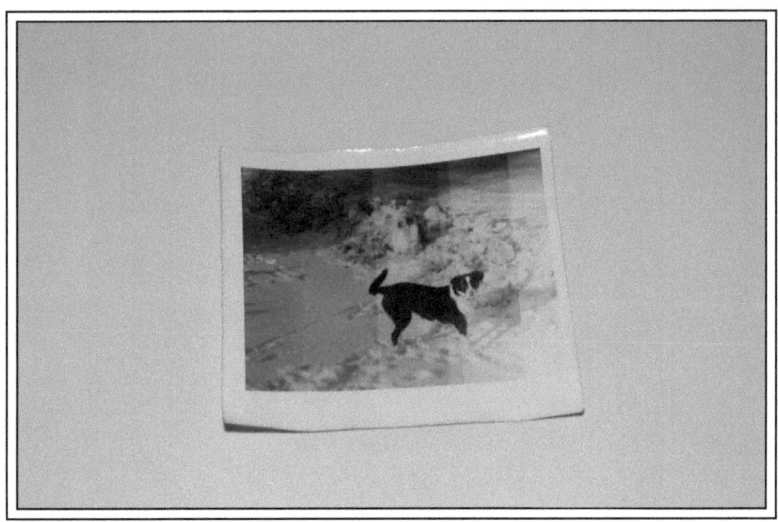

Whitey (My Dog)

This picture was taken around 1965. Taken on a Polaroid Instamatic camera. State of the art technology then.

NOTE: I have only one picture of my beloved dog "Whitey", who was an integral part of my family as I/we grew up. I will be extremely surprised if any of my brothers have any pictures of Whitey, and they will be thrilled to get a copy. (Sorry brother Buzz, for making you cry when you see this.)

When you are finished sorting, you should have a pile or piles of photos something like this.

19

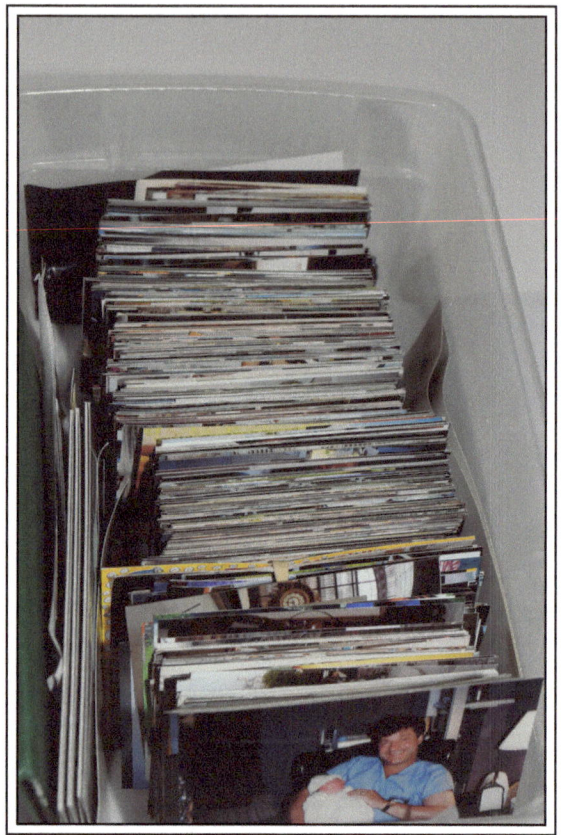

My Box of Keepers

Pile 2: **A pile of pictures and content that may not be easily scanned.**

For example, very old and brittle pictures, pictures in current albums that may be damaged if taken out of the album, press clippings, recipes etc., or some pictures that have one or two good components. Keep in mind that a horrible picture of the entire family may have a great shot of a single member within it that can and probably should be saved and digitally edited. This is easy and inexpensive to do. So, pay attention to what you purge.

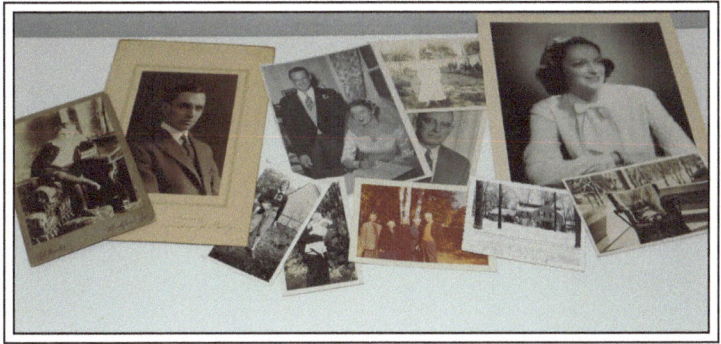

Photos and fragile items that need special individual attention.

Pile 3: Consider also a gifting pile.

Some pictures may not be important to you, but could be priceless to others. Make a big pile, then re-sort these later for gifting to individuals. Trust me they will thank you. These make great gifts.

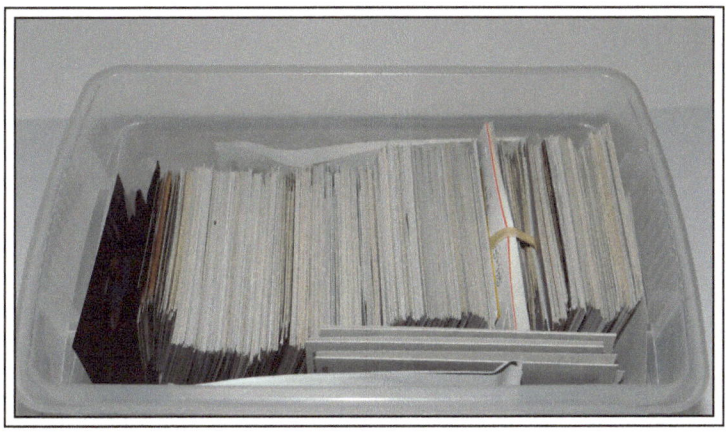

Gifting or Crafts Pile

A great idea that I learned from my Aunt Jane: Make little cards out of a piece of a picture. She would cut out a picture of a person, punch a hole in it, put a piece of string through the hole and write a note on it. This is perfect for labeling Christmas presents. Crafty, yes. Fun, yes. Clever, yes. Very memorable. Use your imagination.

Pile 4: **Recycle / Trash.**

Throw out ALL of the bad pictures! (Out of focus, no theme, people you cannot identify.) Purge ruthlessly! Shred if the content is of a personal or sensitive nature. (IF you wouldn't show it to your mother, wife, husband or children - shred it.)

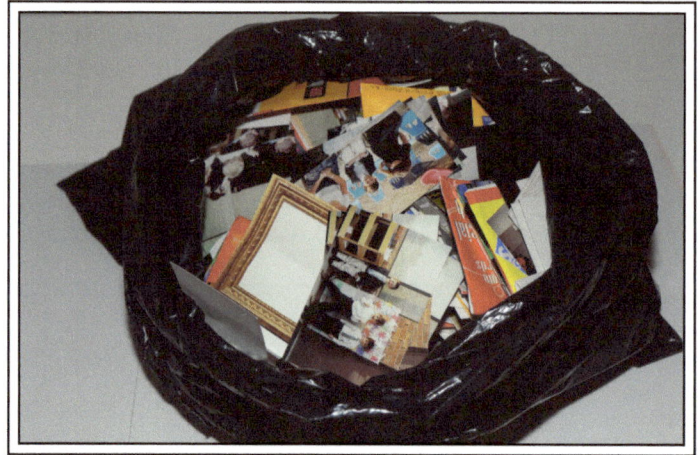

Trash

5

YOUR KEEPERS – Best Pictures

Can you imagine how precious this picture is to me and my family?

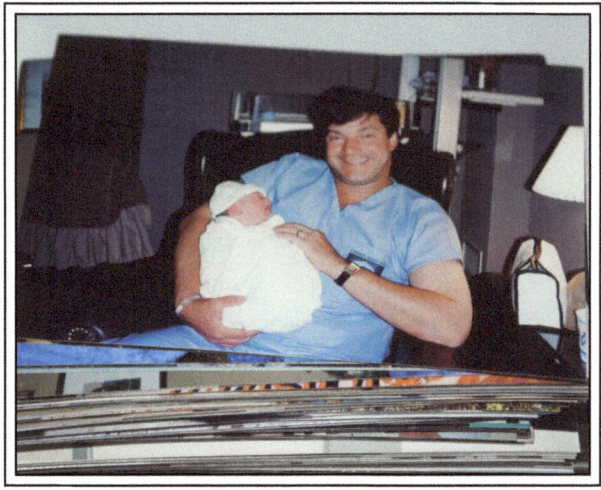

Picture of my daughter, about 2 hours old

You now have your inventory of your Best Pictures. You are ready to convert these into digital form.

Put these in the order you would like them to appear once they are digitized and loaded onto digital media.

Group chronologically by event or by topic.

6

Step Four: Digitize Your Pictures

Now that you have your pictures organized, the next step is digitizing your memories. There are several ways to go about this. Organizing may have been a large job so you may want to turn the digitizing over to professionals or you may want to continue to do it yourself. Once converted to digital, your pictures will be much more usable. They can be easily stored, preserved, viewed, shared and modified easily.

Do it Yourself

Take another picture with your digital camera: This is a very simple way to digitize your hard copy pictures. This will not be a high quality picture. You will however have a digital copy of a cherished memory. I did this when I was home visiting my mother. She has many pictures on a photo wall. I spent five minutes and made digital copies of all of the pictures. Easy, fast, and now I have them to enjoy later

Scanning at home: Scanning is actually very simple. Today, many low cost devices are available, which give you the ability to scan pictures.

A multi purpose device contains a printer, scanner and copier costs less than $100. Models are available at local computer retail stores, or in on-line stores.

Hewlett Packard dominates this market.

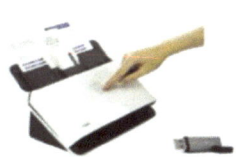

Dedicated scanners are available at retail stores and on-line as well. These are built for the single purpose of scanning images. They will contain software that has many features.

Picture scanners. There is a category of scanners that is specifically designed for pictures.

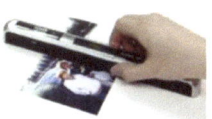

Wand scanner. This is a category of scanners that is small, and portable. These devices will allow you to scan pictures, and other objects.

Most scanners will generate reasonable quality results. The more you pay for a specific device, the better results you can expect. This can be labor intensive however, having pro- 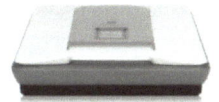 vided a space for the project, you can scan your photos a few at a time at your convenience. Some scanners have an auto load feature that allows you to load a great many pictures to be scanned at once. Perhaps up to as many as 50 or more.

NOTE: For the purposes of this book, I cannot go into exact details for each and every scanner and how to use them, or how to manipulate the resultant digital files. Most are very easy to use and come with specific directions for their use.

As a general rule, the process is as follows: Once the scanner is connected to a computer, software specific to the scanner will automatically "Load" itself and configure itself to the specific system. If you encounter problems, you will need to read through the manuals, and/or, contact the scanner's technical support group for help.

Once the scanner is functional, a picture or image will be placed into the scanner. Some scanners have the ability to scan several pictures at the same time. The machine will perform a scan, or in other words it will read the item, convert the information to a digital format, and notify the system that a digital file is ready to be received. There is usually a prompt from the system asking you what you want to do with the file. At this point, you will need to pick a name and a folder to store the file. You more than likely have the option to choose the format in which you can store the file. That is up to you, it is usually achieved by choosing from a menu of options.

You now have your picture in digital form, and can treat it just like your other digital pictures or objects.

When you digitize your photos, you have several choices as to where to store them --- CDs, DVDs, memory sticks (also called "Thumb Drives"), BlueRay disks or on your hard drive.

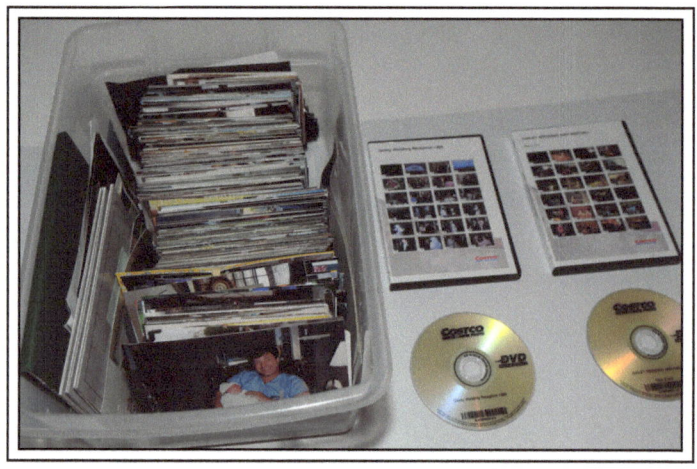

Picture of the DVD / BlueRay with Pictures

26

> *Tip:* A standard CD will hold approximately 2,000 high quality pictures. A DVD will hold approximately 15,000 high quality pictures.

Your first copy of your digitized pictures should be considered you're "Master." In the example above it would be a "Master Disk." Make at least two copies of that "Master" disk so you can store one in a safe place, a safe deposit box, for instance. Keep a third copy of the "Master" at home as a "Working Master."

Using Kiosk Scanners

Currently several large retail stores have photo departments, and/ or kiosks available that will allow you to use their digital scanners for a nominal fee. Some charge by the number of scans. Others will only charge you for the media you buy to store your photos.

> *Tip:* A drawback to kiosk scanners is that this is very time consuming and there may be other customers in line. Depending on the size of your project, you might not be able to complete your entire project in one trip.

Find a service to do the scanning

You can elect to let the photo department do the scanning for you, saving time and effort. Most retail firms that process pictures have services that will do the scanning and digitization for you. Prices vary so shop around.

Follow any of these options and you are ready to start to enjoy your valuable memories, heirlooms, histories and stories. Keep the original hard copy photos in a safe place. They are irreplaceable. Work with the digital versions whenever possible.

Services to do this digitization can cost as little as $.15 per picture to much more. It depends on who does the digitization, what level of quality you chose, and how many pictures you will convert. These services are readily available at camera stores, and at most large drug stores in the US and Canada.

Tip: As you add more pictures to your library, periodically make copies of all your photos. Create a new set of "Master" copies and put at least one in a remote "Safe Place", far away from the working copies. If and when disaster strikes (Fire, flood, tornado etc..) you will feel safe in knowing that you have a full set of all of your pictures in that remote spot out of harms way.

Photo Negatives

Follow the same processes described so far for all of your photo negatives. Services are available to convert and digitize your negatives. The same service providers may offer the service to convert negatives to digital formats. Call and ask about those services. It is possible to get a much higher resolution digital file from a negative. Again, check with the service provider for the details.

7

Step Five: Upload Digital Pictures To Computer

Upload the digital pictures to your photo files on your system.

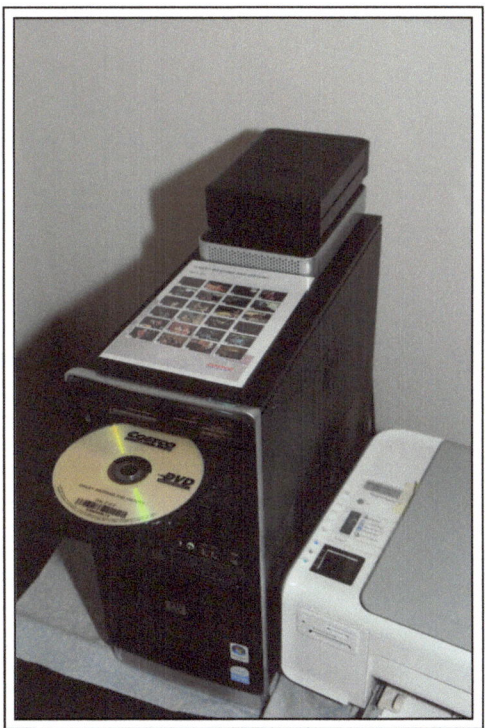

Uploading the pictures from the CD, or DVD to a PC

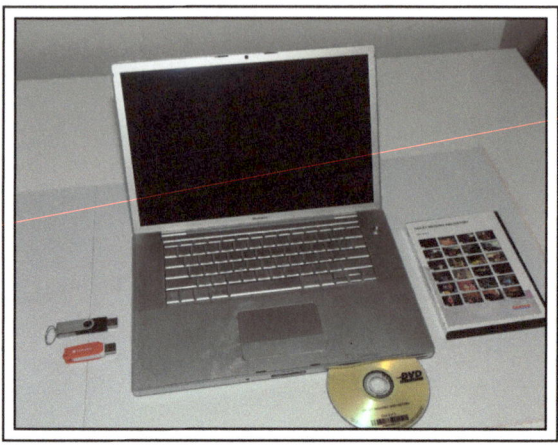

Uploading the DVD and/or thumb drives to a notebook.

Consider uploading photos to an on-line service.

Very Important!

Do not rely on the on-line services for your **entire** storage and preservation strategy for this data!

NOTE: It is my personal opinion that the "On-Line" services are not mature enough to guarantee the safety of these precious personal assets.

8

Step Six: Backup & Preservation Strategy

Maintain your digital photos as part of your ongoing back-up and preservation strategy. Create and follow a simple routine called a Hierarchal Storage Management (HSM) strategy!! Data is considered to be the most valuable asset in big companies and their data centers. There are detailed processes to back-up, copy, secure and preserve data.

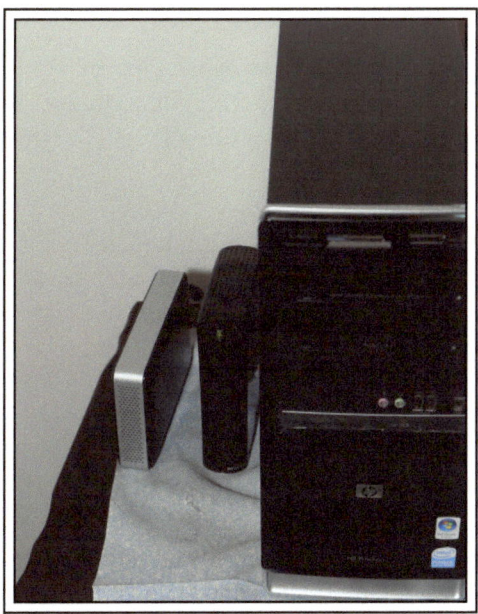

HSM Strategy – System with two external drives.

Two External Drives. Copy all pictures in your system to BOTH drives. Notice this is a 4-year-old PC system.

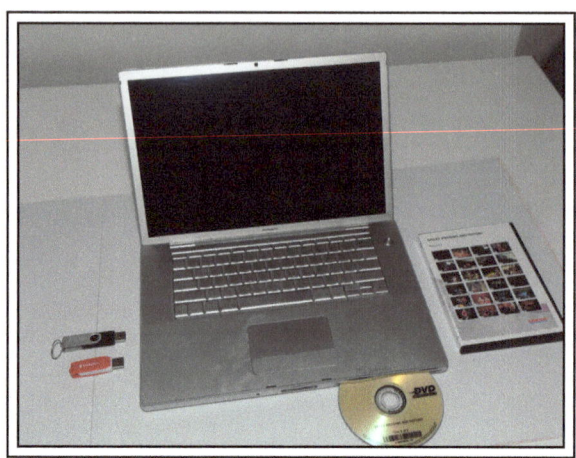

HSM Strategy – System (Notebook) with two external "Thumb Drives, OR CDs, OR DVDs.

How you do this all depends on what type of system you have, and what type of backup media you chose to use. Each has cost issues. A simple explanation of a three level Hierarchy strategy is as follows:

Level 1: Transactional data that you are changing all the time. Your individual pictures will not likely change. But your entire library of pictures will change as you add more pictures to it, or delete pictures.

Level 2: A copy of all of your data at any given point in time. This is also called a "snapshot" of your data, much like a snapshot picture. It is a point in time that you make a copy of all of your data. At that instant, you will have two copies. That is important should something happen to your level 1 data. Keep this data locally with your computer on separate media such as an add-on external disk drive, or on a CD, DVD, or BlueRay, depending on how much data you have and what media you decide to use.

I highly recommend a separate "Add-On" Disk Drive. Less than $100 each. These are small devices 3 ½ inches by 5 inches by ½ inch.

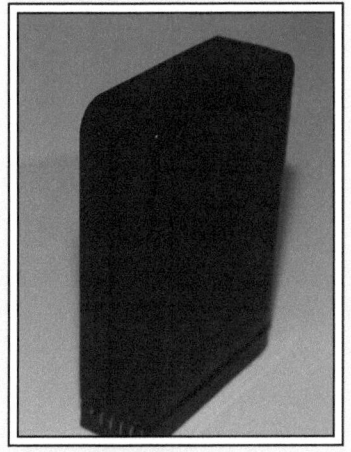

NOTE: There are nuances in some definitions here. An "internal disk drive" is a storage device that is imbedded within your PC or notebook. An "external add-on disk drive" is in an enclosure that will sit outside of your system and is connected with cables. There is a category of "external disk drives" that are called "portable drives" These are external drives that have a more rugged enclosure, and can withstand a bit more shock and vibration than other external drives. Depending on how large your files are and how many times you will be physically moving the external disk drives around is how you should make your decisions. The point is to have multiple copies of your data so if something happens to one, the information is still available on the others.

Level 3: A copy of level 2 data. Stored on a different "Add-On External" device or media type. Now you have three copies. A better thing! Take that third copy and move it to a safe place; a safe deposit box if you have one, or a fireproof safe. The farther away you move this copy geographically, the better. You hopefully will not need immediate access to this copy. Make extra sure it is safe and remote. Consider this a very inexpensive insurance policy for your pictures, and other data.

Why do this?

Computer systems lose data. Disk drives "Crash". Things happen. Houses get flooded, or burn down. Earthquakes and tornados happen. (The US has averaged over 1,300 tornadoes per year the past 5 years.) Many things beyond your control happen that threaten your data. So, have a plan. If your system crashes, use the local back up copy. If your house burns down, get the copy from the safe place and reconstruct your files. (In this case your pictures.)

VERY IMPORTANT!

Every so often, make it a point to back up your system via a snapshot back-up. Do this for all of your data. Not just your pictures. Your pictures will be a sub-set of your data. The routine that you should follow is simple.

Back up all of your data on the local "Add-On" drive, or CD, or DVD, or BlueRay. Take that backup copy and go to your remote safe place and switch it out with the one that is stored there. Take that remote copy, and back up your system again on that media. So you have in effect switched the copies out. Updated both. Now you have three fresh copies of your data. A good thing.

You have a decision to make. How often do you need to do this? Only you can decide that. Keep in mind that if catastrophe strikes, the data that has been changed between the times you perform this routine last, will more than likely be lost. So do it regularly, at least once every three months. Every month is better. Every week is better still. Some folks do this every day. If you follow this advice your photos and data will be safe, secure, and preserved for a long time.

IMPORTANT TIP

One little test for you: Make sure that after you think you have made those copies, go into the destination drive or media and open a few files. In other words, confirm that the data was actually copied.

The "Cloud" option:

Consider using internet based services for backup. BUT they should be **ONLY A PART OF YOUR STRATEGY, NOT YOUR ENTIRE STRATEGY!** There are many services to choose from. Make this "part" of your strategy, NOT your entire backup and preservation strategy.

Once the hard copy photos are digitized they can be edited, catalogued, and placed into digital albums that can be easily shared and displayed. Software and or services are readily available to work with these digitally formatted photos. The ideas are endless and easy to create: Family albums with multiple generations, vacation photos from the past, sports teams, chronicling a journey, events.

9

Step Seven: Create Albums to Share

Now that you have your photo library organized and digitized, the following are suggestions of what you can do with it.

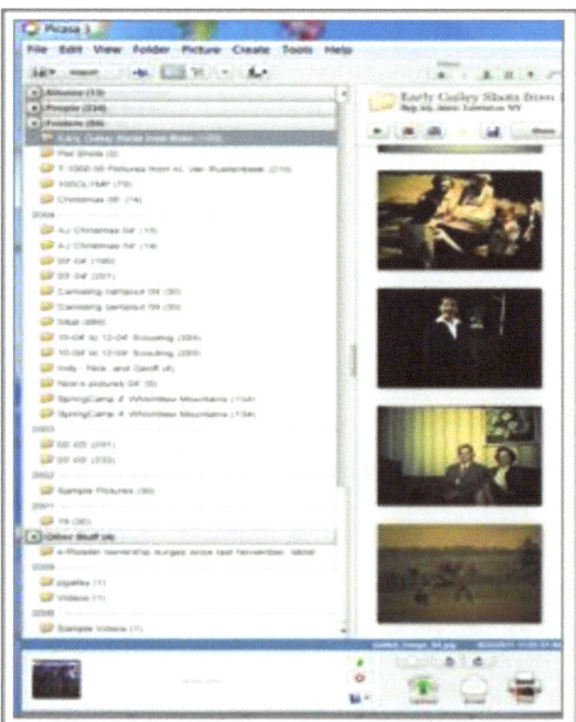

Photo albums in Google Picasa.

Many different options are available to you once you are organized, and many are free.

Some examples include: Scrapbooking, hard copy photo books, story books, digital albums, slide shows, sharing content over the internet, creating special event albums for anniversaries, family histories, special occasions. The list is limited only by your imagination. You can chose to use the originals or print out high resolution copies from the digital files.

Scrapbooking — This is a very large industry. Most craft stores have aisles dedicated to scrapbooking with clever ideas to make your books memorable and unique. Once your photos are in digital form, they can easily be manipulated. For example, they can be resized, made into black and white, and modified with editing tools. The results will give you many more options and flexibility in your scrap booking efforts.

*Hard Copy Photo Book*s — There are firms that produce hard copy books in a "Print on Demand" basis.

Story Books — Story books can be created with many themes that are available in the craft stores, or on-line.

Digital Albums — Many services are available on the internet that will allow for the creation and the sharing of digital albums. Simply go to a browser and search for "Digital albums" and you will have many resources. I use Google Picasa, Facebook, and Flicker to name a few. These are all free services.

Slide Shows — Once a digital album is created, it is simple to make a slide show. There is usually an option to view the digital album in "Slide Show Mode". You can also download the digital album onto removable media such as a CD, DVD, or "Thumb drive" and take the album with you. Simply insert the media into a system and you have the ability to see your album either as individual pictures, or as a slide show. Most Internet Service providers that have photo services will allow you to share your photos individually, or as a group in a slide show.

Albums can be created around any topic you chose. Great examples include: Weddings, Graduations, Family Get-togethers, Children, Anniversaries, Sporting Events, Teams, Special Occasions, Journeys, Travel, Histories, Memories. The list is endless.

10

Your Digital Photo Strategy

The process of organizing photos you've taken on your digital camera is much the same.

Follow the same process above. With digital photos, the process may be a lot easier. There are many different tools like Google Picasa which help organize, edit and share your digital photos. The size of the effort depends on the number of pictures you have.

Six years ago my 80-year-old mother had the great idea to gather all of the old slides of our family and have them digitized and put on a VHS tape. She presented a copy of the tape to each living family member. Quite a treat!

Recently, I had that VHS tape converted to DVD format. It is a prized possession. Very nostalgic, and invaluable to me.

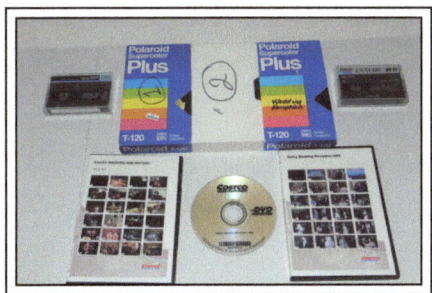

VHS format converted to DVD format.

The cost to convert from VHS to DVD is nominal. All the family shots and the copy of my wedding video and reception was money well spent!

Your Digital Photo Library

The process is much the same. Repeat all the above steps except those covered in chapter 6. Gather together and consolidate, categorize, sort, save, purge, share, and finally preserve with a local pro-actively managed HSM strategy.

11

Enjoy and Share Your Pictures

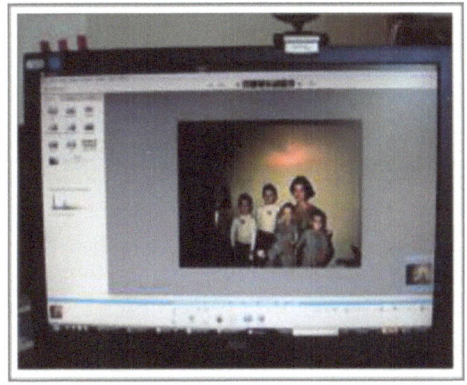

Family picture from 1958 viewed on a PC.

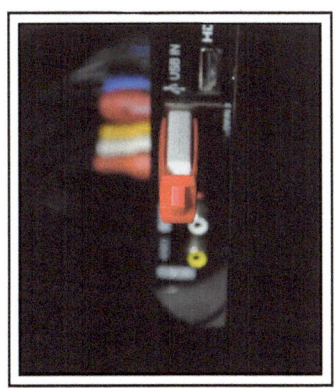

Thumb Drive attached to an HD TV

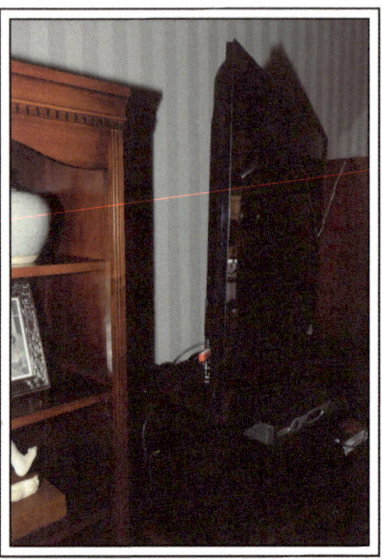

Thumb Drive attached to view a photo slide show.

Most current television sets and monitors have the ability to accept a "Thumb Drive." Copy your cherished pictures and watch them in a slideshow on your viewing devices. This can be done on a PC, notebook, tablet, photo frame, phone and/ or a television set.

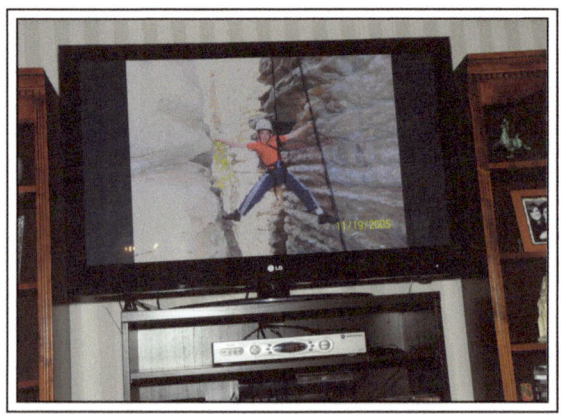

Picture of my son on an HDTV via a "Thumb Drive"

Share electronically. Make cards and albums and send pictures. Have some fun with the electronic tools available to manipulate this content. Invite your family and friends to enjoy them with you!

You have now completed the process. You started with a pile of disorganized pictures, and now have an organized structure and way of using, sharing preserving and most important of all, enjoying your most valued pictures.

12

Going Forward
Leveraging technology options

Technology will allow for many options that were not available in the past. New technologies will give you even more options in the future.

Once your images are in digital form, they can be enjoyed in many different ways. Consider the range from a digital key chain to the giant monitor at Times Square in New York City and anything in between. It is easy to carry your entire digital library on a thumb drive, DVD, a notebook computer and or a tablet. Today you can purchase a digital picture frame that will store and show a large digital photo album.

Depending on how advanced your computer skills are, it is relatively easy to create and share a digital slide show with music in the background, and commentary throughout the show. This is particularly easy with software tools like iMovie on the Apple platform and Windows movie maker.

Edit with abandon. Consider that the best time to perform the high level sorting, purging, and editing is probably before you transfer from your camera, or phone to your system.

I recommend keeping only the good high quality photos. Purge the rest before they get to be clutter. Save the best photos to your system. Create new albums and enjoy and share them. Incorporate the albums and individual pictures into your back-up and preservation, strategy covered in chapter 8.

Remember to keep the original hard copy photos in a safe place. They are irreplaceable. Work with the digital versions whenever possible.

Once you have a digital copy, it is easily replicated and shared. Create digital albums that can be shared. Either make a copy on physical media, and send it to someone, or make an album that can be shared on-line in many of the photo sharing services.

In Conclusion:

Keep in mind, your volume of pictures will not shrink without a proactive effort on your part. This comes down to a very personal set of decisions. No one knows what memories are important to you as an individual. You will need to make these decisions yourself.

The Process:

1. Gather and consolidate your hard copy photos.

2. Organize your photos chronologically.

3. Sort and purge the volumes to a manageable volume.

4. Digitize your inventory.

5. Create and execute a digital back-up, archival, and preservation strategy.

6. Create a strategy to enjoy your pictures.

7. Share your pictures.

8. Follow the same process and techniques with your digital pictures.

Use new technologies as they develop. Migrate your pictures to the newest technology. (For example VHS to DVD migration.) Do not rely on any one single technology or service to copy, secure and preserve your pictures and data. Technologies become obsolete quickly. Usually, about every five years there is a new replacement technology that will obsolete prior technologies.

Consider incorporating Internet based services to supplement your strategy. These are great tools to share pictures.

It is not yet clear if these services are reliable enough to use as primary preservation services. Figure out the nuances of the Hierarchal Storage Management (HSM) strategy, and incorporate in your every day life.

Finally, please send me your feedback, and any observations via the website www.PIMCoach.com.

Acknowledgments

Many sincere thanks go out to scores of people that have helped me with this book. First and foremost is my wife Robin who is my constant supporter and companion.

A big thank you also to Andy Howell my main editor who provided great advice during the early stages of this book. Thanks to Robin for the cover art. Major supporters during the development of this work include Mike Short, Dennis O'Hagan, Alan Feigenbaum, Charlotte Moore, Debbie Bidwell, James Lee, Laura Scherer and Sue Latham.

A special thank you to Gary Spinell, for his support as an accountability partner, coach and mentor.

Thanks also goes out to the great work being done by Charlotte Moore and Rita Dear of the DFW Independent Publishers of Dallas Meet-up group.

Learn More

Want more information on Personal Information Management and the topics of "Taming the Data Deluge" as it relates to your personal life?

On-line resources:

For a list of observations and solutions that relate to everyday Personal Information Management issues go to:
http://www.PIMCoach.com

Follow the PIMCoach on Facebook by hitting "Like"
http://www.facebook.com/PersonalInformationManagement-Coach

Follow PIMCoach.com on **Twitter@PIMCoach**

Add my Google+ page to your circles. Search for "PIM Coach"

Have a question? Please visit:
www.PIMCoach.com/have-a-question/

Quick Order Form

Email orders for more copies of this book are available at: Peter@
PIMCoach.com Quantity: 25 50 100 250 500+

Call for volume pricing: 214-336-1286

Complete and e-mail this form

Name: _____

Address:_____

City, state/Province, Postal Code: _____

Tel: _____

Email:_____

Payment: Check: Visa, Master Card, Optima, AMEX, Discover

Card Number: _____

Name on Card: _____

Exp. Date: (mm/yy)_____

Satisfaction guaranteed: I understand I may return any item for a
full refund with no questions asked, for a period of 60 days from
original shipment data.

See our website www.PIMCoach.com for information on other books, seminars and topics concerning Personal Information
Management and how to: "Tame the Data Deluge".